ROOMS

PHOTOGRAPHS *by* DERRY MOORE

Text CARL SKOGGARD

Editor JOSEPH HOLTZMAN

Managing Editor & Text Editor PAUL B. FRANKLIN
Art Director, Nest Books TOM BECKHAM

nestbooks
RIZZOLI
NEW YORK

First published in the United States of America
by Rizzoli International Publications, Inc.
300 Park Avenue South, New York, NY 10010
www.rizzoliusa.com

© 2006 Joseph Holtzman
© Compilation Derry Moore

2006 2007 2008 2009 / 10 9 8 7 6 5 4 3 2 1

Printed in Italy

ISBN-13: 978-0-8478-2826-5
ISBN-10: 0-8478-2826-3

Library of Congress Control Number: 2006926593

You might say that Derry Moore has his special way with a room. Joseph Holtzman, the guiding spirit behind *Rooms*, is convinced. Having watched Moore shoot many interiors during the last ten or twelve years, it is his belief that the photographer can make himself comfortable in any domestic setting. Within a very short time, he situates himself, finding the best perch from which to contemplate his surroundings. He works quietly and efficiently, with the least equipment possible, so that watching him you feel that he should be able to do his job without even disturbing things. He is highly adaptable, never formulaic in his camera angles. He knows precisely when to take his shot to seize the always (it would seem) fleeting light. Derry Moore's at-oneness with his rooms comes across in photographs that are definitive. To put it simply, he is the very best around at doing what he does: capturing sophisticated, usually traditional, often aristocratic interiors.

Straightforwardly titled, the present survey is itself straightforward. At least we hope you will find it so. Altogether, images of rooms from two dozen houses and apartments dating from between 1975 and 2005 and spanning nearly the whole of Moore's distinguished career have been included. They comprise a unique collection and point to the privileged access that Moore has always enjoyed as the Earl of Drogheda and as the son of parents who were at the center of the London cultural establishment. In person, he is winning, the soul of politeness. (I do not think that he can ever have been thrown off a location.) These images are intended to evoke Moore's idiom, not so much to provide a documentation of settings; indeed, some are mere glimpses. But we think that, invariably, they suggest something essential about each place, even as they demonstrate his uncommon talents.

The chronological sequence adopted for *Rooms* mimics the conventional retrospective exhibition. The photographs have been presented as the works of art they are, uncropped and marginless and free of captions. Because every single photograph was originally in square format, the book you hold in your hands is square, too. Surely Moore counts as one of the outstanding practitioners of square composition; even his rectangular photographs are often implicitly square as compositions and look their best when cropped to be literally so. In keeping with the evocative, occasionally even mysterious nature of the images selected for *Rooms* are companion texts, one per feature; they are intended to supply a verbal counterpoint to the images, responses in kind. Dispensing here and there information about Moore's persons and places, they remain impractical in the best sense of that much maligned word.

If we were to ask what is the essential thing about Moore, the short answer would be that he refuses to interpose himself between subject and viewer. Rather than act as an interpreter, he likes to assume the role of an appreciator. The role calls for consummate tact, yet without any pretense of photographic "objectivity." For the appreciator must always be consulting his own highly developed aesthetic sense. Moore, who is never intimidated by grandeur, finds the human dimension, the subtle comforts and humble pleasures that lurk in the most imposing of rooms. He is charmed by forlorn glamour and by the strains of exoticism persisting in the corners of his world. And although he appreciates rooms that argue on behalf of a refined and harmonious European "high culture," he would instantly tell you that what really fascinates him are the odd brews he has discovered farther afield, above all in India (which he visits regularly).

Wherever he happens to be, Moore looks to atmosphere and to the qualities of surface—those chief contributors of poetry in any room. Much recent domestic photography depends on artificial lighting to produce the heightened effects of chiaroscuro, i.e., dramas of its own making. Moore prefers to rely on natural light or at least to evoke it, and in this he is a real master. His light, falling upon the objects in a room, gives expression to the whole spectrum of materials to be found there. They are encouraged to speak as do, say, props in a well-rendered Dutch still life. Moore's sensibility runs counter to the current fashion for bleaching out the incidents of surface in favor of the lineaments of pure (designed) space. He himself says that he expects to find in a room "wonderful color sense, extraordinary proportions, and sympathetic light." He believes that one is both "surprised and soothed" by a truly remarkable interior.

Moore might have spoken of "character" as well. For in one way or another, the rooms he has tackled are rooms that possess, or did at the time possess, this quality. We feel that their characters were formed by varying circumstances. Some of the rooms shown here are the handiwork of professional decorators, of leading lights in the field in fact—Elsie de Wolfe, Nancy Lancaster, Madeleine Castaing, Renzo

Mongiardino. Except for the last-named, however, their rooms were not conceived for a client, but for their own use. (Thus, even in our "decorator's rooms," one sees an unattenuated reflex of personal taste rather than its management.) Others of our rooms evolved with little professional assistance or none. Or with the help of interior specialists long gone, so that the residue of centuries lies over their interventions. Indeed, by far the greater number of the twenty-four sites chosen for this book ought to be regarded as old or venerable, and of these, a majority are now being preserved for their historical and aesthetic value. Besides De Wolfe's classic Versailles pavilion, Villa Trianon, there is a Tuscan country house nearly five hundred years old; a fortified urban house in Castile some seven hundred years old; Hôtel Lambert, the greatest Paris townhouse erected during the long reign of Louis XIV; and a Welsh garden nearly as old and belonging to a castle that had been in existence for almost half a millennium before the garden was laid out. Several of the "newer" houses may claim historical importance as well: Charleston, the modest rural retreat of Bloomsbury's artists and intellectuals, and Villa Otto Wagner, a prime instance of Viennese protomodernism from the 1880s.

The geographical distribution of our sites offers a rough, no doubt incomplete reflection of Derry Moore's professional rovings. His heartland would appear to be France (seven sites) and England (five). Spain, Italy, Austria, the United States, and India each supply two abodes, whereas Wales and Ireland round out the list with one apiece. As many as eight of the twenty-four sites are genuinely rural; our country houses range from mighty Chatsworth in Derbyshire, England, with its several acres of roofs and thirty-five thousand acres of land, down to a queer little house and garden in the south of France owned by a witch (one man's opinion). Three of our features are as much about a garden as a house, and we have one princely hunting lodge in Austria stuffed with antlers. Two-thirds of the interiors are (or were) to be found in towns and villages or in large cities—Paris, London, New York, Madrid, Vienna, Turin, Dublin, Hyderabad. Unsurprisingly, all four decorator's projects in our survey were done in a great city or its environs.

Of the homes documented, some, maybe one-third, might be regarded as "ancestral," that is, as principal residences which have been held by a single family over the generations. (Falaknuma, the huge palace in Hyderabad which fell to the

Sixth Nizam shortly after it was built, does not qualify because even though his family continued to own it until quite recently, only one generation ever lived there.) Ancestral residences, whether in towns or in the countryside, tend to preserve the efforts of earlier generations, yielding the equivalent of exposed geological strata. Perhaps it may serve to speak not merely of character but of a "domestic micro-culture," if the term can refer to the ongoing adjustments and compensations, to the dynamics that arise when styles and possessions mingle in a house over long stretches of time. The acculturation in such places, viewed through Moore's camera, may strike us as having been a gentle process, because of his ability to evoke their rich patinas. We may even fancy that their appropriations have been unconscious, although this is a fancy that really does not withstand interrogation. Probably there were struggles aplenty over matters of taste in these residences, of which we can know nothing. At any rate, Derry Moore's photographs suggest that old interiors, no matter how eccentric or grand, undergo a seasoning that blends together the fugitive passions, the pretensions and snobberies, the appeals to fads and foreignness, that would have drawn attention to themselves when they were fresh.

Over and against the ancestral residences are other old houses that have experienced vicissitudes in ownership, among them Hôtel Lambert, which would eventually be purchased by Guy and Marie-Hélène de Rothschild, and, of course, Villa Trianon. For our purposes, these two are to be distinguished from the temporary living arrangements devised by apartment dwellers and the owners of second homes only by the magnificence of their "bones." In common with the latter run of places, which include the apartments of Pauline de Rothschild, Nancy Lancaster, Lady Diana Cooper, Rudolf Nureyev, Madeleine Castaing, and Joseph Holtzman as well as houses owned by Tassilo von Fürstenberg, Lulu de Waldner, Michael Casey, and the Reverend Peter Gomes, they have been fashioned according to the vision of an individual or the requirements of one or two generations of a family. (We must omit the summer home of the Duchess de Mouchy from this roster.)

Some latecomers, Gomes for example, are very wise concerning the charms of an ancestral home. His carefully appointed New England interior, he knows, could never compete with one evolving as the "accumulation of generations of mixed taste and abilities, the whole…greater than the sum of its parts." Nevertheless, most

in the latter group have sought, sometimes with nomadic cunning, to achieve the ripeness of a kind of past. Some, like the recent owners of Hôtel Lambert, have spent enormous sums of their own reviving vanished sumptuosities. Some, like Joseph Holtzman, play against expectation in a spirit of humor and irony, knowing as they do the impossibility of it all. Some, like Nancy Lancaster and her partner, John Fowler, have been serious and systematic about their nostalgia and businesslike in the bargain. (Now that modernism, too, has revealed itself as another historical style, there can be no escaping our reckoning with some past or other.)

Many of the features in *Rooms* come with one or more portraits of the inhabitant or inhabitants of the place. With the passage of time, Moore has devoted himself increasingly to portraiture, but as we see from the review of his work here, he was always ready to commemorate people along with their houses. And indeed, if rooms are characters in their way, so are people—especially when they are framed by their rooms. Some of his portraits count as farewells: We show the decorator Renzo Mongiardino lounging in a tomblike subterranean bath of his design, less than a month before his death; Madame Castaing is a marvel of preservation at age ninety-six, two years before her death; and Lady Diana Cooper, truly the "Lady Di" of her day, a jaunty wonder of ninety or so, two years before hers. We did not go much younger than the forty-seven-year-old Rudolf Nureyev, but he may have been moribund in two haunting images Derry Moore made of him in 1985.

In some cases, a modern habitation survives its inhabitant, but most do not. Among the very beautiful rooms recorded here and which are no more, we ought to mention those created by Pauline de Rothschild; gone as well are the interiors designed for Rudolf Nureyev and Diana Cooper; even Elsie de Wolfe's Villa Trianon now houses a cultural institute, while the palace of Falaknuma shall be a tourist hotel. The newly resplendent raiment of Hôtel Lambert captured by Moore was shed as recently as 2005. The oddities of Charleston survive, admittedly, and so, too, does Nancy Lancaster's Yellow Room (as part of the premises of Colefax and Fowler). And yet one wonders—Can preserving rooms in state, with their contents and less their people, yield anything other than benign paralysis?

ROOMS

"YOUR HOUSE IS ENCHANTING"

Be advised, dear reader, that many of the truly extraordinary palaces of the world are to be found in India. When Great Britain imposed peace on the Subcontinent in 1858, the local princes and kings—rajas and maharajas—ceased warring against one another and turned instead to conspicuous consumption, perhaps the most splendidly conspicuous ever known. And that was for the good. Where poverty is widely shared and there is no shame in being poor, ostentation on the part of the well-off few becomes public entertainment, a benefaction shared in by all, legitimation of things as they happen to be.

The sprawling marble-clad pile of Falaknuma—one of Derry Moore's early Indian subjects and perhaps his favorite—lies a few miles outside Hyderabad in south central India. It sits amid formal grounds on an arid boulder-strewn rise; a muddy river meanders below in the middle distance. Some say that a French architect whose name is forgotten erected Falaknuma circa 1872, taking seven years, while others bestow the honor upon equally unspecified English architects. In view of how grand this place is, their vagueness seems odd. Here, wings project from either end of a massive central block for hundreds of meters, further than those of Buckingham Palace. Falaknuma's adaptation to local circumstances shows up in deep double-story loggias (offering great expanses of shade) and a wealth of ornament. Nevertheless, its exterior remains eclectically European and nineteenth-century.

These photographs were taken in the 1970s. At the time, Falaknuma's interiors, also European, were unaltered from the late nineteenth and early twentieth centuries. Save for utilitarian improvements such as overhead electric fans, rooms had not been renovated since shortly before the First World War.

Like other overweening establishments, Falaknuma had known glory but for a day. Fate lay in wait, albeit patiently, from the first. Its commissioner, a brother-in-law of the Sixth Nizam of Hyderabad, found himself obliged to turn the house over to the Nizam himself after that ruler was gracious enough to pay a visit and express his favorable opinion. And since highborn sons of Hyderabad were always called upon to build their own residences rather than occupy one in which a father has died, Falaknuma was dealt another blow with the death of the old Nizam in 1911. Left untenanted by the proprietary family, it served merely as a place to receive visiting dignitaries. Through long years of afterlife the palace was punctually swept and cleaned and dusted; minimal repairs were made. Such attentions, scrupulous though they undoubtedly were, might have been cruel except for the fact that Falaknuma's gentle, irresistible ageing created an incomparable patina. Silk hangings decayed (without crumbling to dust) and wool carpets went bald, as did the Victorian plush, producing strange haloes. Paints and dyes faded and grew ethereal. In Moore's magical images, such changes are to be read against the near permanence of wood, stone, porcelain, and glass, which simple housekeeping could keep fresh.

The spell is now broken, however. India itself is stirring, shaking off what has sometimes seemed to outsiders a general enchantment. Falaknuma is being converted into a hotel by the Taj Group. Meanwhile, from their modern house on a nearby hill, descendants of the Sixth Nizam still glimpse the ancestral residence through trees.

PENANCE TRUE

Pauline de Rothschild did not permit many things to share her four rooms in the Albany, that venerable edifice at the corner of Piccadilly and Old Bond Street in London where she lived from 1969 until her death in 1976. The walls remained bare except for one or two mirrors, one or two paintings. Over the mantel in her husband's bedroom, one of these very few paintings, a Japanese portrait on glass of a Chinese courtesan, was suspended from a fancifully furrowed silk ribbon. Two wisps of teacups held down either end of this mantel; there was also a small and simple bedside table supporting plain brass candlestick lamps with paper shades (and on the floor before the fireplace, another such lamp and shade), and a wicker waste can. A little armchair lurked just inside the door. Philippe de Rothschild's chinoiserie four-poster with tester and curtains of silver and black brocade (the fabric turned inside out to yield ghosts of floral imagery) might have filled half the room, yet it only made another frame for the lofty window, the sunlight streaming in. Plumped, double-ruffled pillows (John Fowler's touch) might have lent a sensuous note, but these sleeping quarters seemed content to be a luminous empty vessel. They did not want a substantial inhabitant. Such, at least, is the story Derry Moore tells with his camera.

Pauline herself (born Potter) slept upright on a narrow William and Mary daybed, semi-invalid. The splendid full-length figure of Elizabeth Montagu in the role of Venus attended by Cupid and two doves kept her company; otherwise, her bedroom was spare. Pauline as a younger woman had passed through the hands of many glamorous men; she had lived very well. Now she communicated across the threshold with a Restoration beauty who may have reminded her of an earlier self (even as her playboy husband dallied with a long-dead minx from half a world away).

Are we in the presence of ascetics? Perhaps. Some people, particularly if they happen to be one-time voluptuaries, enjoy a more complicated relationship with the sumptuous than do you or I. Pauline's cleverly dressed, choice eighteenth-century chairs and her scatter rugs of skin and fur were floating in the Albany like rafts of fugitives borne away on the flood. Retour d'Egypte chairs in fruitwood gilded and mounted with ebonized heads of sphinxes kept staring back through time, beyond anything we can see. If there was to be a future in this place, a promise of life to come, it was in the light admitted through exuberantly curtained windows. Here at last was something that would not fail.

Here is another Indian house; another from Hyderabad, in fact, in photographs dating back a quarter century. Derry Moore says that few men will ever be more polite and more hospitable than a particularly polite and hospitable Muslim aristocrat hailing from that city. The paterfamilias in these sweet and decorous images of domesticity was just that sort of man, he adds.

At first glance, the furnishings in Nawab Zainul Abidin Khan's parlor may remind you of a middle-class English interior, circa 1925, without the modern miracles of cabinet radio and phonograph player. (Whether such things appear in any more recent photos, we do not know.) Vitrines and whatnots are bearing their usual freight of little vases and mementos; serviceable upholstered armchairs carry the allotted fringe; and a fancy glass candelabrum surmounts the circular marble-topped center table with faux rococo legs in some sober dark wood. Altogether, quite a cozy atmosphere and not even the floral carpet is missing.

Look once more, though, and it will be obvious that this could never be England or the home of English people of one class or another. What do you make, for example, of the walls casually arrayed with framed likenesses and scenes, plates of various sizes, and the other oddments worked in here and there? And what of the colors? Somber if not dull greens, yellows, and grays are not everyone's idea of cheerful or subtle, or whatever it is that is desirable for your inmost refuge. The windows must be few or shuttered, and in the family parlor, it is positively gloomy (gloom gathering beneath a high ceiling). What doors there are would seem to be kept permanently open, with passageways left lightly curtained. Strangely, those leading from the parlor are decked with grand matching gilded pediments reminiscent of Spanish Baroque frames. In another room—a sporting milieu to judge from the antlers and the swarm of equestrian portraits—pigeons cluck and coo their way toward the middle of the plain stone floor.

In fact, the rooms and furnishings, though Anglophile, are perfectly and unpretentiously Indian: The Nawab's appropriations are innocent. Unreasonably, the murk of the parlor, the palpable atmosphere, suggests Vermeer to me, even as I remain quite confident that cloistered private life does not flourish here. When not posing for Derry Moore, surely the family and dependents of the Nawab become animated and garrulous. Radio and Victrola—CDs and television—are rarely missed when voices

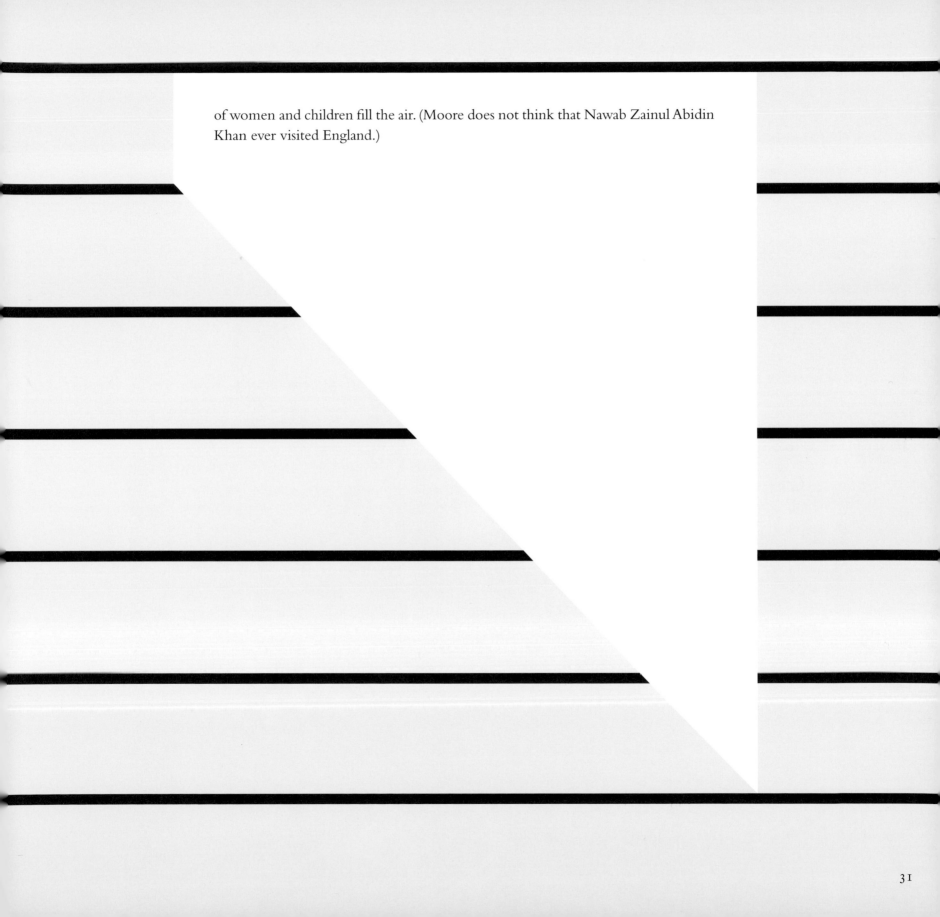

of women and children fill the air. (Moore does not think that Nawab Zainul Abidin Khan ever visited England.)

MASTER OF THE HUNT

This hunting lodge, formerly the possession of Prince Tassilo von Fürstenberg, is another of those settings which appear to have escaped alteration; such places exercise their own fascination and arouse our curiosity. Certainly Prince Tassilo, named for an eighth-century strongman who had held the Bavarian territories and who, having wavered in his loyalty to the King of the Franks, was forced to relinquish them and withdraw to a monastery, was a fixture among the Austrian nobility. He could trace his lineage back to the eleventh century. Yet he did not inherit his family's wealth (which went instead to an uncle). We might suspect that he was unable to afford any refurbishment of his modest lodge, but seeing as he did mend his fortunes through marriages to impressively rich women (an Agnelli, a Texan), the suspicion can be laid to rest. Perhaps the prince liked the lodge just as he found it. (Moore observes that here was a man's lair if ever there was one.) Two children by his first wife ended up movers and shakers in the international world of fashion; one wonders what effect the old place may have had on Ira and Egon, and whether, paradoxically, it may even have inspired them.

I am informed that Prince Tassilo was a member of the pre–jet set of the 1940s and 1950s. Furthermore, that he was usually in pursuit of some woman or other. It is easy to imagine him taking refuge from that sort of chase and retiring every so often to the lodge on the Wolfgangsee with men friends. The generous paneling and buff walls are in absolute tonal sympathy with whiskey and tobacco. Though whether the prince himself led hunting parties productive of the trophies which came to line his corridors like a natural cornice and prick out the walls of his study with a sort of three-dimensional wallpaper, I do not know. These images, taken by Moore in 1979, are mum. Perhaps his subject did not engage in sport at all. Perhaps, God forbid, we are witnesses to the methodical industry of a forgotten Austro-Hungarian decorator, a specialist in rigging up such lodges with suitable remains. (Recall Vladimir Putin's astonishment when he suggested to his friend George Bush that the two of them saddle up for a ride around the ranch, only to be told that his host could not ride a horse at all.) What we do know is that creatures of every element, of the air as well as of the land and the waters, contributed body parts to the miscellaneous bounty. And that the imperishable Alps would have always been on hand as faithful retainers to make sense of any activity one would think of undertaking.

43

It seems an impertinence to write anything about Charleston, the iconic venue of proper English bohemianism. By now everyone knows all there is to know.

Recently, or at any rate since our photos, both house and grounds have been spiffed up—restored—and hosts of people visit during the set hours. They see all there is to see. Among other things, they inspect the orchard, sheer wilderness when Quentin Bell, aged eight or nine, ventured in and found John Maynard Keynes, hidden from the social business of the place, meditating what would become *The Economic Consequences of the Peace*. "I shall tell them that the Germans can't pay more money than they have," the great man is supposed to have told the child, thinking of Versailles. (One year before, cannon fire on the Western Front had been rattling the windows.)

A favorite spot with visitors is the walled garden. Down the years, its exuberant hues, borrowed from Matisse and Bonnard, seemed never to fail Charleston's painters. (At Charleston, whoever wanted could pick up a brush, and as we know, many did.) Quentin's mother, Vanessa, the most devoted of these painters, and perhaps the best among them, would be remembered by Quentin as she sat distraught amid the profusion of the garden at summer's height in 1937, not long after her eldest, Julian, had been ambushed and killed while driving an ambulance for the Spanish Loyalists. Everyone knows about that, and about how her sister, Virginia, came over almost daily during that summer from nearby Rodmell to comfort her. This was four summers before Virginia, fearing Hitler was about to invade, famously filled up her pockets with rocks and drowned herself in the River Ouse, not far from her house. Everyone on the Sussex downs in those days knew, of course, that the German invasion would find them sitting ducks, but on the whole Charlestonians preferred a country refuge to London and bombing raids. The amenities of a new bathroom, water mains, and electricity all came to the house to cheer those who made it their year-round residence for the duration of the conflict.

Everybody surely knows of the pretzel of sex and love at Charleston and the way sometimes it turned into a Möbius strip. Look no further than Angelica, Vanessa's daughter, who ended up marrying David Garnett, Vanessa's lover's lover or, if you prefer simplicity, her father's lover. When Derry Moore photographed the place in

53

the late 1970s, Angelica, Garnett, and Duncan Grant, her father (or her husband's ex, which is the same thing), were mainstays of an ageing establishment. Moore, who still casts his eyes heavenward in praise of Charleston's morning coffee, recalls neither Duncan nor his daughter being "unduly fussed about bathing" and qualifies the domestic conditions then obtaining as "doubtful." His images of the Garden Room (with a bay window looking out to the flowers) show good-natured decorations a trifle complacent, a little down at the heels; certainly these figures and patterns (laid on in various epochs by Vanessa and Duncan) are without pretension or any thought for permanence. Admirable indeed are the hybrid fireplace/ovens devised by the critic and painter Roger Fry (occasional lover of Vanessa, highly regarded as well for his writings on Cézanne). They manage to conduct heat out into a room without sacrificing the charm of an open blaze; one was installed during the very first Bloomsbury winter at Charleston, 1916–17.

A STYLE IS BORN

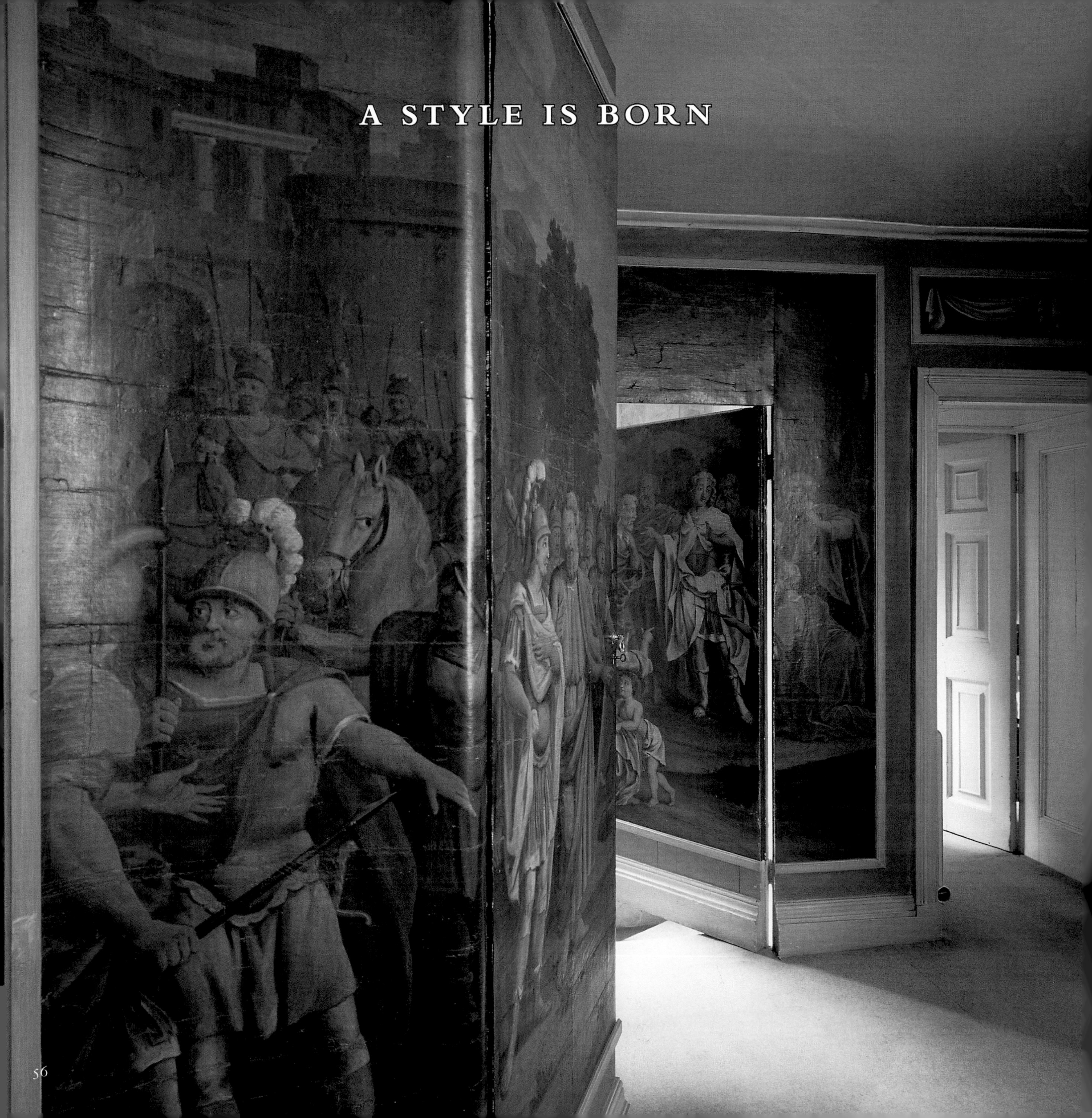

Nancy Lancaster has gone down in history, decorating history that is, as the founder of English Country House Style—which style she and her close associate, John Fowler, promoted through the business she owned from 1944, Colefax and Fowler. Today, the Colefax Group is a huge enterprise, but pickings were slim in the early days. One heard that the socialite from Virginia and the professional artisan from Bedford Park squabbled so much that they might have been the most unhappily married couple in London. Still, theirs was a labor of love. She had been born in the year 1897 in a cottage on her grandfather's plantation, Mirador, near Charlottesville. The family, well-connected and socially ambitious, was just regaining its footing after the evils of the Civil War when Lancaster came along. Bedford Park, Fowler's birthplace in London, was quite another story, a community in the spirit of the Aesthetic Movement of the 1870s, the world's first garden suburb, its original houses done in the self-conscious, precious Queen Anne Revival manner. Bedford Park would provide an instant haven for artists, architects, and designers and was even touted by that hard-to-please gentleman William Morris.

Whatever their differences in background, the inventors of the Country House Style (we prefer the plural) shared a nostalgia for romantic pasts. Hers had depended on slavery and was struggling to revive itself through a combination of elbow grease and Southern chutzpah. (Lancaster's beloved grandfather, who eventually managed to make millions through railroad contracts, still clung somehow to the old adage that work was "for Yankees and Negroes.") John Fowler, one surmises, would have liked to pretend that the Industrial Revolution and all its dingy works had never been. Their great opportunity came as the decline of the English landed classes turned into a rout with World War II. Country House Style would make a virtue out of necessity: If old furniture had to be covered in chintz instead of being reupholstered, then that material would be elevated—and the more faded, the better. The quality of one's furnishings was a neutral datum; fine pieces were cherished, of course, but the Country House Style could do with modest ones provided they had enough flair. It could even do with mean rooms, as Nancy Lancaster demonstrated with her last home, the tiny Coach House (actually a former cart shed) on the property of Haseley Court, the magnificent Oxfordshire house which she gave up for a loss after a catastrophic fire in 1971. The Coach House made

it clear that Country House Style would surround you with charm no matter what your circumstances. Only brand new was banished.

Derry Moore's photos are of quarters for Nancy Lancaster carved from a portion of the Colefax and Fowler premises in Mayfair in a renovation begun in 1957 and destined to yield the most celebrated interior decoration in modern England. Originally, the structure had sheltered horses; then, circa 1800, Sir Jeffry Wyatville created a large studio on the uppermost floor. Lancaster and Fowler transformed Wyatville's handsomely proportioned, vaulted space into a sitting room/dining room/library/office that would be known as the Yellow Room. It was Fowler who applied so many layers of glaze over stippled-on Peking (or butter) yellow paint that these walls shimmer as few walls can ever have shimmered in centuries past. A crowded sort of comfort was achieved with furnishings brought from Lancaster's other residences. Only the curtains and Venetian-style chandeliers copied from a pair in Charles de Beistegui's palazzo were fabricated for the Yellow Room.

Here you have English Country House Style at high noon in the heart of the metropolis. Some of the more imposing things, for example the full-length portrait of one Mary Fitton (1578–1647), would have been introduced after the dismantling of Haseley Court, though it should be understood that the Yellow Room does not and never did depend upon the pedigree of its furnishings. (Fitton is alleged to have been the Dark Lady of Shakespeare's sonnets.) Since Nancy Lancaster's death, at the age of ninety-six, the room has been treated by Colefax and Fowler as a shrine which any customer may visit at will.

"FERDUSI" TO HIS FRIENDS

Once Derry Moore had acquired a taste for Indian houses, he began searching for something closer to home that might excite his interest in the same way. And it turned out that Spain was ready to comply. Standing in an Edwardian-era garage entrance to the palace of the Marqués de Casa Torres, Moore felt the old enchantment. Here, in the heart of Madrid, as though by everyday agreement, were the Marqués's no-nonsense black sedan (nicely buffed and polished) and, just twenty paces behind and equally at your service, his medieval knight in armor leaning forward on a plaster mount (somewhat worse for wear). A magnificent incongruity worthy of India.

As it happened, Moore was obliged to make the best of an opportunity on the spot, and spent several hours that day documenting what he could of the Marqués's endless establishment. These images date from only two years before the expiry of the Marqués, in 1984. Don Fernando de Aragón y Carrillo de Albornoz was of the school of yesteryear, a courtly bachelor absorbed in his social round and, in the words of our informant, a "very sweet old boy." Little had altered in his house since the Great War, or at least that is the impression it made. Most remarkable of all were the Marqués's noble salon (surely the least pretentious interior in the world) and his bath/dressing room and bedroom. You will be struck by the simplicity, verging on austerity, of his places of retirement, notwithstanding their scattering of Goya drawings and small adornments.

The old man's bed, in particular, can only have been outdone by the thin, hard military cot which sufficed for Franz Josef, last of the Austrian emperors but one. (Our own taste for extravagant bedrooms, and still more for the sybaritic bathroom, would appear to be compensation for our living and dining rooms, sites facing extinction.)

Suitably, the Marqués de Casa Torres was heir to and custodian of one of the great private collections of Spanish paintings. Paintings and drawings mingled with his cumbersome ancient furniture throughout the house on Calle Fernando el Santo; a few were on hand to greet you in the garage. One would like to think of these as boon companions, even intimates. The experts pronounced it an "uneven" collection, but did that matter? Over the years they came and went, the experts, inspecting this or that Velázquez. Upon his death, the Marqués—"Ferdusi" to his friends, an allusion to the celebrated Persian poet, though sometimes he was no more than "Ferdy"—gave three masterworks to the Prado. The rest of the art was parceled out among his relations, one of them being Fabiola, Queen of the Belgians, third daughter of Don Gonzalo Mora Fernandez Riera del Olmo, Marqués de Casa Riera, Conde de Mora and Doña Blanca de Aragón y Carrillo de Albornoz Barroeta-Aldamar y Elio. How revealing are names to those who know how to read them.

I suppose that if any house ever did, this one had good bones. Elsie de Wolfe and her longtime companion, the theater agent Elisabeth Marbury, would have seized on the fact at once, after peeping through the iron grille on the Boulevard Saint-Antoine in Versailles. It was just over a century ago; Anglo-American tastemakers were busy declaring war on the suffocating interiors of the Gilded Age and claiming pre-Revolutionary aristocratic France as their Zion. Villa Trianon, perfect in its dainty way, might have been made to order. Formerly, the little pavilion had belonged to the second son of Louis-Philippe, the "citizen king" who abdicated his throne during the Inconvenience of 1848. It was a genuine fixer-upper, and de Wolfe's sympathies were as fiercely engaged as could be. In her autobiography *After All* she would write that it made her think of "a beautiful woman who had had a tragic history and who had grown worn and faded before her time."

In the event, she spared no effort to restore and refurbish Villa Trianon. It became a monument to her sense of style and, for the remainder of her life, a well-lived-in home and a powerful draw for society and fashion. At bottom, de Wolfe was the innovator who figured out how to create a chic and easy modern house with those good bones and just enough other ingredients borrowed from Marie Antoinette. Her own mirrored pilasters and doors and signature leopard-print throw pillows blend effortlessly with the polite furnishings of that precarious era. She may have been almost too successful; at any rate, de Wolfe's ideas have been thoroughly assimilated and the originality of her style can be difficult for a casual observer to detect today, when everyone appreciates the bones and believes in eclecticism.

Our images, taken thirty-two years after de Wolfe's death and shortly before the contents of Villa Trianon were sold, give pride of place to her bath and bedroom. These intimate spaces appear deceptively fresh. The bedroom, measuring only ten by seven feet and lined with painted parcel-gilt boiseries, harbors many delicate works of art, among them a *Madonna and Child* by one of the Tiepolos. For her bath, the small and spirited woman created a new kind of room altogether, making it into a cozy sitting room with fine old wallpaper, comfortable chairs, and eighteenth-century Chinese églomisé paintings. But every room in Villa Trianon shows her remarkably sure touch. It is owing to Elsie de Wolfe's artistry that we sense nothing whatsoever of the just-so perfectionism with which French interiors are often

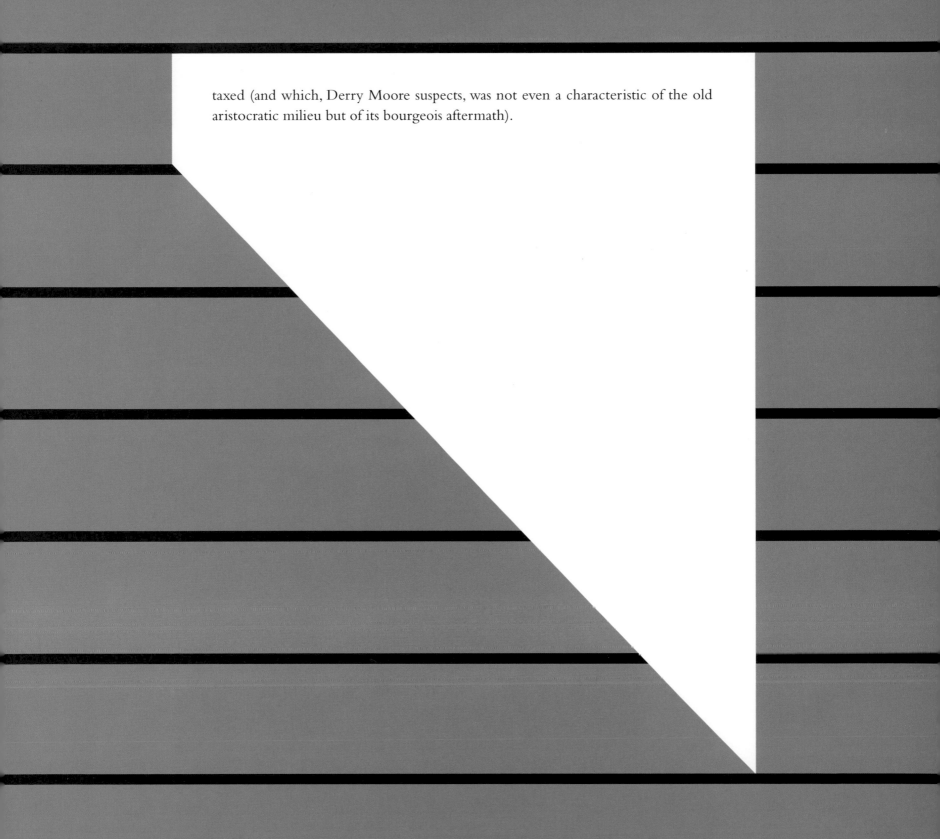

taxed (and which, Derry Moore suspects, was not even a characteristic of the old aristocratic milieu but of its bourgeois aftermath).

92

HER LAST LIE DOWN

Marie de la Rochefoucauld, Duchess de Mouchy, died "in the most wonderful way," says Derry Moore. "Came in from her flowers, went for a lie down, and was found dead two hours later." The lucky duchess was known far and wide for her inventive gardening, which she practiced for more than thirty years between June and October on her not overly large property near Paris. Here, French garden formalities and English garden freedoms met, qualifying each other; or perhaps they were secretly in league. House and garden lay behind high walls and were invisible from the village street. Entering by means of a carriage entrance cut in the walls, one discovered a sinuous fleur-de-lis of yews stretching toward the flank of her two-story, ivied farmhouse. Upon one of her graveled paths winding beneath a canopy of magnolias and deep feathery cedars, you might come up against a slab of boxwood with a slender arched perforation for your passage. There were a number of such fanciful portals and everywhere the duchess's topiary was ingenious. Her shapes could be witty—instantly recognizable—as in the case of her row of yews impersonating orange trees in tubs—or enigmatic. The penguin-like, more than slightly phallic figures growing close by her house made one wonder if she were simply pulling your leg. Without meaning to imply gloominess, I should compare her fancies in the remoter turnings of that garden landscape to those of an affluent cemetery which is not groomed to death. (People do seem to venture more with their mausoleums than with ordinary dwellings.)

Duchess de Mouchy's rooms were again playful and, above all, organic. Things arrived in her farmhouse either as inheritances from one or another of the branches of her very grand family or as flea-market finds. Both seemed to be natural processes of accumulation. Once you became an object in her house, of course, there was no telling the company you'd be placed with. Say you happened to be a postcard: The duchess might insert you in some precious old frame to hang between a pair of her ancestors. Lesser keepsakes, each with a history she liked to relate, could be anywhere. Duchess de Mouchy's sense of tone was infallible, her arranging of furniture superbly effective and not the least contrived. The red in her own bedroom, for example, was just enough in quantity and quality to make this an absolutely satisfying "red room" (though one would just as soon find quietus in her blue room). We might, if so inclined, regard this woman in the capacity of a decorator, but why should we? Really, if more among us had her authority and skill, there would scarcely be any need for decorators. Moore made portraits not only of the duchess but also of her butler/gardener—who is remembered for having served him an ambrosial breakfast—and an archetypal housekeeper.

IT WAS NOBLESSE OBLIGE

114

Derry Moore enticed this subject to pose in her large, slightly Hollywoodish canopy bed. Quite possibly it was not difficult for him to manage; Lady Diana Cooper, after all, was used to the limelight and had a reputation for naughtiness and bravado. Many thought her the most beautiful Englishwoman of her day. Born Diana Manners, the daughter of a duke, she had traveled with the fastest of the Edwardian fast set, but never became a really "bad" girl like Nancy Cunard. She acted in silent films during the 1920s and toured America with Max Reinhardt as the star of his epic pantomime, *Miracle*, taking the role of Mary, the Mother of God. In the wake of that stage triumph, Cecil Beaton (who must have adored her) created images of Lady Diana as a mock-sacred celebrity in religious attire. And silent film seems still to haunt Moore's bedroom portrait.

The young ninety-something is also shown seated before bits of trompe-l'oeil painting that Rex Whistler devised for her in 1935. In addition to such oddments as playing cards and medallions suspended from cords (casting shadows), Whistler furnished his client with two masterworks of mendacity—simulations of Poussin and Claude Lorrain (*Offering for Diana* and *Diana the Huntress*). Gower Street, where Lady Diana chose to spend her widowhood, had been resplendently bohemian during the 1930s when the decorations were done. These whimsy-filled rooms must have faded very gently, along with Lady Diana, who never could, of course, fade altogether. Moore remembers her wonderful eyes.

I should say that Diana and her coterie were entitled to their frivolities. Males among her early friends, aesthetes nearly every one, tended to die on the Western Front. In 1919, she herself married a hard-living, literary-minded war hero whom she had learned to know as the school friend of her brother John. Alfred Duff Cooper was to become a close associate of Winston Churchill and, as the outstanding dissenter from a policy of appeasement, resigned from the Chamberlain cabinet after Munich. In 1944, he was named ambassador to liberated France, where he and Diana spent much time afterward. Husband and wife each went on to write autobiographies indispensable for understanding their age of hectic amusement and gallantry. It is an experience certain to elude our cautious, self-centered, earnestly egalitarian one.

At Chatsworth, staterooms occupy the uppermost floor and command magnificent views. However, these grand rooms, attained by means of two flights of steep stairs, have often failed of favor. "I was never more disappointed," wrote Horace Walpole after visiting Chatsworth in 1760. The Gothic novelist found its staterooms in particular to suffer from unrelieved gloom and inadequate furnishings. "A museum of old furniture and a walk in bad weather," judged the Sixth Duke of Devonshire, the "Bachelor Duke" who began a costly renovation of Chatsworth during the Regency. Sad to say, few besides royalty have ever stayed in the Great Apartment, as this suite of rooms is known. It actually takes up the site of the main gallery in the Elizabethan forerunner of the present house and would seem best suited for the display of paintings.

The real domestic quarters at Chatsworth—which has always been in the hands of a single family, the Cavendishes—are scattered throughout the enormous house; the family's receiving rooms lie on the first floor, so to speak "below stairs." Their estate was acquired in 1549, when that quintessential female alpha, Bess of Hardwick (then styled Elizabeth Cavendish), urged her husband to the purchase. The title of Duke of Devonshire was created for the bold Cavendish who was among those to welcome William of Orange to England in 1688. The First Duke of Devonshire must surely have dreamed of receiving his new patron in the Great Apartment of the house he was rebuilding up from its foundations. Yet I find no trace of such an interlude.

So far, there have been an even dozen Dukes of Devonshire, all of whom have dwelt at Chatsworth. Derry Moore's photographs record the livable side of Chatsworth as fitted up by Deborah, wife of the Eleventh Duke. She is proud to have done the job herself, i.e., without the aid of a professional decorator, but as the editor of our volume wishes to point out, she had quite a reasonable supply of furnishings and whatnots to play with.

Visitors to Chatsworth are invariably struck by the legacy of the Bachelor Duke. It shines forth in two libraries by Sir Jeffry Wyatville, the larger created from an original long gallery (whose ceiling was kept) and the lesser decorated by Pugin's interiors man, John Gregory Crace. Victorian irreverence enlivens the Bachelor Duke's approving description of his Crace interior as "something between an

illuminated manuscript and a café in the rue de Richelieu." (A fine summation, by the way, of the bandbox fashion of an era.) Deborah, for her part, seems to have preferred chintz, but she did rescue Chatsworth from the brink of dereliction. Appropriated by the government in 1939 and made to serve as a girls' school, it stood empty for twelve years before she and her husband could return to set things right, introducing desperately needed modern improvements. The Duchess (since 2004 Dowager Duchess) proved a formidable entrepreneur whose meat, dairy, and produce operation, Chatsworth Farms, now brings a yearly income of millions of pounds. She is an estimable woman and also deserves our consideration as the last of the six Mitford sisters, and the second-least notorious. The large Sargent in her Blue Drawing Room shows three granddaughters of an earlier Duchess of Devonshire; she herself commissioned several portraits of family members from Lucian Freud and has claimed to be a great fan of Elvis Presley.

WHICH WAY MODERNISM

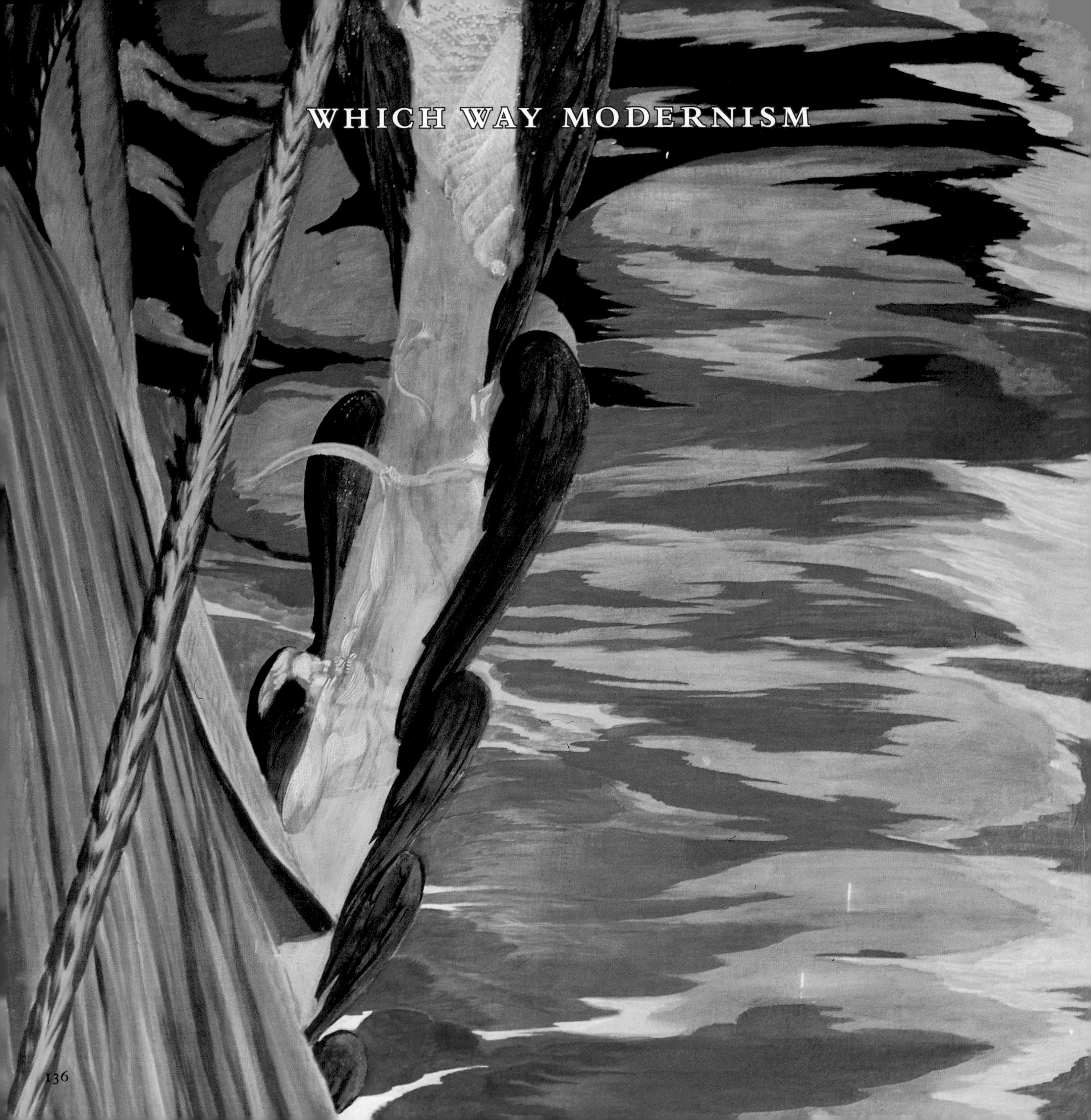

Many of us find the Viennese approach to modernism fascinating or, at least, fascinatingly peculiar. Perhaps that is because we fancy to have departed from modernism along a path resembling the one Vienna once took in getting, or almost getting, there. How strange to be progressing along your own chosen path and encounter the likes of Josef Hoffmann or Otto Wagner forging theirs in the very opposite direction. The neo-Tuscan villa that Wagner built for himself and his family during the years 1886–88 in Hütteldorf, in wooded hills on the western outreaches of Vienna, amounts to a protomodernist riff on a beloved historical model; some postmodernists might, however, indulge in a similar stylization.

Villa Otto Wagner, as the place is known, was quickly recognized as significant. Yet it managed just the same to fall on hard times and had even been slated for demolition when Ernst Fuchs, leader of the Vienna-based art movement known as fantastic realism, took possession in the early 1970s. Here is a man who not only paints but draws, makes prints, sculpts, builds buildings, designs stage sets for Mozart and (Richard) Wagner operas, composes, writes poetry, and sings. And fathers children, eight according to one of my informants and twice that number according to another. In taking over the villa, Fuchs was apparently not in search of a conservator's laurels. Quite the contrary; he has made of it a shrine to his own sensibility, a showcase for his paintings and his decorating. Officially, Villa Otto Wagner has been known as the Ernst Fuchs Museum and open to the public since 1988. Derry Moore's photos date from 1985.

The makeover did not cause Villa Otto Wagner irreparable harm. After all, Viennese modernism's severity was never more than mock severity—a species of mannerism. What we really enjoy, we decadents, is watching this glamorously strained sensibility flirt with kitsch. Fuchs merely exposed further the yearning of Villa Otto Wagner for a locally prized commodity. And what of Fuchs himself? His technique, combining resin oil and egg tempera, emulates Dürer and is nothing if not serious; his subjects are drawn from the great storehouse of world religion and myth and legend. Skipping through that winged mandorla, for instance, is none other than a pixilated Saint Virgil, founder of Christianity in Salzburg. The canvas is in Technicolor, with its smoldering high-Venetian backdrop (rendered respectable by Moore's lighting). Fuchs has something about him of the successful up-to-date shaman. Should you encounter him along your chosen path, you might consider resetting your time-travel clock.

THE DANCER

Nureyev, seated on his Russian sofa covered in Caucasian kilims, poses not once but twice for you. The portraits were taken in the dining room/library of his Paris apartment when he was forty-seven years old. For one whose leonine presence had electrified men and women time and again, he is curiously swaddled, a bit like the fledgling that puffs itself up against an ill wind. Yet, though he looks to be freezing, he still smolders. Derry Moore supposed he was suffering from a cold, and Nureyev was a collector of costumes and textiles. That he himself suspected anything more than a cold appears improbable; the latest infiltrator of our blood was just losing its cover in 1985.

Meanwhile, the etymology for the word *handsome* has always seemed to me to show good solid sense. The earliest traceable meanings, "ready to hand" or "easy to handle," used in connection with objects of use, made the slightest of transits before attaching themselves to the likes of Rudolf Nureyev. After all, doesn't the *handsome* man strike you as functionally superb, as someone you are dying to get your hands on? These Paris rooms, conceived with the help of Renzo Mongiardino's associate Emilio Carcano, were as tactile as Nureyev himself. Dark Cordova leather stamped with a rich floral motif spread across the living room walls; plump back-to-back sofas, clad in silk and Genoese velvet, cried out for one's hand. And as if to reward etymological conjecture, Nureyev devoted the walls of his dining room/library to academic studies of the male nude for your glance to graze upon.

The rooms were sumptuous and yet restrained, rich in their sobriety, theatrical in a sort of masculine way. One esteems the choice of a severe chandelier for the living room and the fact that it held real candles. And also how the reflections of those candles would have shimmered around the cornice mirroring and glinted from gilded tracery of an admirable Gothic simplicity. And even how a robust Hermes, luxurious tresses spilling out from beneath his stylish helmet, peered innocently in the direction of a sweetly armored (distinctly older) gentleman propped against the mantel. It was all said most succinctly in the bath, where an acrid, perhaps poisonous green set the tone. Artificial gleams from a fake skylight fell upon sinister walls, upon the great dancer's deep copper tub—more dramatic than Marat's—and upon a folly of handsome faucets and tubing which, for its operation, must have required the bather or someone to stand at attention. Or so I picture it.

PERFECT AS PERFECT CAN BE

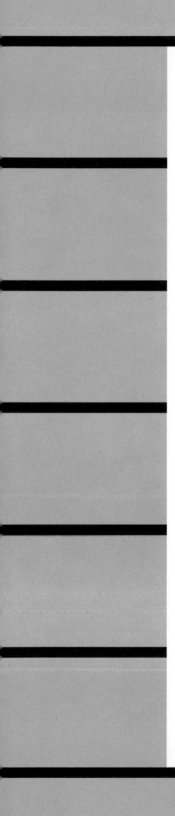

The trim classical chateau of Le Fresne, near Tours, is one of those perfect French houses. In speaking of its perfection, we refer to all but timeless massing and proportions, and to the enduring rightness of its interiors. Yet every work of our hands expresses a certain time and place, a particular mentality; Le Fresne is no exception. Completed in 1770, a fashionable commission for the heir of a purveyor of hats to the King, Le Fresne (Le Frêne, "The Ash") seems the very embodiment of its time and place. In the aftermath of the French Revolution, the estate passed to a weaver's son grown rich as a mercenary in India. Its present owner, Paul de Brantes, claims descent from that mercenary (and that weaver).

The photographs of Le Fresne taken by Derry Moore are among his best. They capture the superb tone prevailing at the chateau, beneficiary of two hundred years now of tranquil custodianship and, as real-estate lingo has it, single-family ownership. In every room, one senses an orchestration of light and surface, a precisely calculated mingling of glint and gleam and gloom. Each room manages to register a multitude of hues that remain in thrall to some master shade. The rooms of Le Fresne, to be sure, do not represent a simple state of preservation; change has usually been welcome as long as it was harmonious. So we find plush Victorian armchairs and sofas conversing amiably with Empire uprights in the salon, and the plainest of plain modern lampshades consorting with a Beauvais tapestry.

To enjoy the beauties of Le Fresne and not think about what they mean would be to err. For however beguiling, they do offer moral lessons. (And so we come back to the idea of perfection, and to time and place.) When this chateau was designed, intimacy was percolating through the domestic arrangements made for the affluent and sophisticated of France. Here, you will find no effort to intimidate by means of a display of grandeur (or false grandeur). Nothing overawes through size. Were the proprietor to adopt even a hint of the seigneurial manner with his guests, it would misfire. More than anything else, more even than refinement, the rooms and furnishings of Le Fresne bespeak good manners; they are meant to nurture kindness in us and a kindly awareness of our companions. A marooned philosophe eager to earn his bread might claim that Le Fresne and its unforced elegance express the unfeigned goodness of dispositions naturally moral. (It is all so simple, really.)

LE GOÛT ROTHSCHILD

Behold the noblest townhouse to rise in Paris under Louis XIV. We are speaking of Hôtel Lambert, completed in 1644 for the financier Jean-Baptiste Lambert de Thorigny. Here, three chief protagonists of Versailles—the architect Le Vau and the painters Le Sueur and Le Brun—collaborated for the first time and here, miraculously, the French Baroque interior flowered in an instant. Sited on the eastern tip of Île Saint-Louis, this house could not lie any nearer the heart of Paris. Nor has society ever strayed far from it. Voltaire quartered himself here (a letter of 1739 to Frederick the Great proclaims Hôtel Lambert to be "the very house for a sovereign who would also be a philosopher"), and here as well, George Sand and Delacroix were guests after émigré Polish aristocrats took possession a century later, give or take several years. Eventually, a Rothschild would reign amid its grandeurs.

The modern Lambert era took shape from Alexis de Redé, the suave man posing in Derry Moore's photograph. Born into an Austrian-Jewish banking family, he reached manhood with a title but no inheritance to speak of. Redé, however, became the protégé of a South American guano magnate and in 1949 found himself established in a suite of Lambert rooms while most of Paris still reeled from the aftereffects of war. These rooms he refurbished in *grand-siècle* style as the setting for a glamorous social life. And it seems Redé had the run of the place: During his memorable Oriental Ball of 1969, for example, half-naked men dressed as Nubian slaves bearing torches lined the stairs leading to the principal floor, and turbaned figures mounted a pair of enormous papier-mâché pachyderms in the courtyard. On other occasions, there were dinners in the celebrated Galerie de Hercule (the inspiration for the Hall of Mirrors at Versailles). It was not for nothing that Nancy Mitford dubbed Redé "la Pompadour de nos jours."

Baron de Redé remained the soul of Hôtel Lambert for more than fifty years, prospering mightily. With the death of his protector, he received half of the guano fortune (a wife taking the other half). The truly great moment arrived in 1975, however, when Redé persuaded his close friend Baroness Marie-Hélène de Rothschild to purchase Hôtel Lambert outright from the Czartoryski family (who were holding on all this time). Thereafter, the "goût Rothschild"—that virtual marriage of the sumptuous and the intimate—was applied liberally throughout, replacing what had been, reportedly, an indifferent eighteenth-century interior.

Redé maintained his old suite within the new Rothschild domain while completing the Lambert restoration and installing in each room Rothschild family treasures gathered in over the centuries from every corner of Europe. To him and no one else, we owe perhaps the most spectacular exhibition ever of Rothschild taste. Shortly before his death in 2004, Redé was named Commandeur des Arts et Lettres by the French government for his contribution to culture. Of course, he would occupy his suite at Hôtel Lambert until the very end, growing a trifle lonely (Baroness Rothschild having preceded him in death). Moore's photos document the house returned to its full bloom, anno 1988.

We yews are getting on. One hundred thousand suns ago, maybe longer, you laid us out here along the garden walks and flights. For a time we were kept dainty and trim. In those days, the terraces still stood out bare against the hillside, the red of the retaining walls punctuated by little else than apple and pear trees measured out at regular intervals and trained against them. Visitors who meandered in the full light along gentle paths next to the parterres, or climbed the steep stairs linking each terrace with a neighbor, took in everything easily enough. Even a child could see over us yews. But who did not feel like a child, in those days? Suppose you should stand on the first terrace. Its breadth and length were liable to swallow you. (People down at the far end peering over the balustrade would seem no bigger than pinky fingers.) Meanwhile, other terraces reared above like steps to the Giant's Castle. Higher still—right over your head—loomed the sheer escarpments of that huge pile which had always been there, even then, the world unthinkable otherwise.

Inside the Castle—but who knew what went on inside? Whoever lived there overlooked everything, oversaw all, and for us that was sufficient. They had been there as long as the Castle had been, which is to say, longer than we could say. On our very first morning, they saw to it that we were watered and clipped. Almost every day, someone clipped away at us, so many men always clipping that we never stretched our limbs heedlessly in some direction that might be pleasing to us. And that is how things went, for thousands of suns: a continual taking from us, an absence of us taking shape for you.

Yet the spectacle of taking from us, the absence of us taking shape for you, eventually ceased to be entertaining. It may be that the ones living above who oversaw everything relaxed their grip on events. Or perhaps we were simply left behind by fashion. However it was, we yews have been shifting for ourselves since. Let those who would know us think of light silently borrowed, from sun after sun after sun— of elements combining secretly within us—of an explosion, though impossibly slow. Now, our shape bears the least recollection of the old laboring against us. Indeed, we have become the overseers of the garden. We tower over you. We blot out the red of terrace walls that no longer stand out bright against the hill. Even the Giant's Castle is ceding its authority to us. You say that we are skewed as our trunks go on twisting and our branches warp with every sun. But the other laborers have tired and turn

away from our shifting. That is the truth, though you prefer to call such yielding a "taste."

Gardens are no simple matter. Ordinarily, we think of them as bowers of innocence, but scarcely have we imagined one when a snake or some other knowledgeable creature will come creeping through a chink in the wall, finding its way inside. Though often we find a woman already presiding over the garden. Such a woman is of course knowledgeable, in possession of magical powers—being an enchantress or worse. And of course, each thing growing in her plot yields its potion, from the delicately branching almond tree to venturesome yarrow with pungent leaves (when bruised) that can be used to clot blood and tell the future.

Possibly I have a witch here in Lulu de Waldner. She shall be simply "Lulu" to you, because these images of her house and garden in Provence urge the familiarity. Witch or not, Lulu gave the impression of being a grownup child, full of purpose.

As for her garden, it was an English garden, near as she could make one. Coaxing such a thing to flower in the land of the mistral, Lulu depended on a trickle of water from a lone artesian well (which she was obliged to find for herself). And to shelter her nurslings from those powerful winds, she built enclosures. Down the gentle slope before her old stone farmhouse trailed a plan of terraces and parterres, hedged and meticulously laid, each nurtured with topsoil and manure brought in by the truckload. In her beds, the plants of England—yew and boxwood, verbena, honey-suckle, and hollyhocks—entered untried alliances with hardy natives at home beneath a broiling sun—rosemary and lavender, cypress, a tiny wild blue iris. Other people in that neck of the woods might content themselves with vineyards—she pursued the quixotic dream of a topiary elephant covered in yellow Lady Banks roses.

It was Lulu's way, after spending the cool of the morning in that willful garden of hers, to carry fresh sprigs and cuttings into the house. Curious arrangements were to be found in every room. Truly, her alchemy of the formal and the fantastic throve indoors, with even stranger and wittier results. No convention governed her match-ing of flower and pot for the "indoor perennial border," her sideboard in the parlor bristling with cups and vases, each holding a bloom or two. Lulu might have been the first person ever to ponder the matter, so artless her matings seem.

Some primordial faith should attend the mounting of dewy corpses in indoor caskets. I do not know what Lulu's was, but she knew how to transform everything. Through obsessive floral patterning, she made her outdoors take up residence within.

On crowded walls, in certain portraits, men assumed the likenesses of beasts. Over that parlor sideboard, she caused a row of horse-head brackets to sprout vegetable headdresses, like the tribesmen in a Hollywood epic. And what, pray, are we to think of her lobotomized Franciscans?

MADAME CASTAING

People have puzzled themselves over Madeleine Castaing's wig, on account of the narrow chinstrap. Why, they ask, in so many words, would anyone resorting to a hairpiece blow his own cover? Looking at the matter through her eyes, though, it appears simple enough. What you see is not a wig but a hat, and no ordinary one at that. Madame is chic, and she has not bothered to hide much of anything. There is pragmatic sanction, too, in the strap's gentle firming up of her chin, which had seen some ninety-six summers when Derry Moore took portraits of her basking away in her office in the warmth of a quaint old free-standing oven.

Her habit in later years was to sit there in her office, at the corner of Rue Jacob and Rue Bonaparte, keeping watch on the traffic in her shop. On occasion, pilgrims came merely to see her. Those who approached the upholstered porter's chair (if that's what it was) were received with distant politeness, for Madame Castaing enjoyed cult status. She had first gone public with her bravura decorating in 1941, during the Occupation. Taking a former laundry in the center of Paris for her commercial premises, Castaing installed completely decorated rooms, an innovation she thought would allow her clients to understand the furnishings she wished to sell. These were indeed unexpected things—seeming freaks from what we should like to call the "in-between times" of the nineteenth century (the general belief then being that a perfect wilderness of taste stretched from the Directoire to Napoléon III). Not only was suspect French material welcome; Biedermeier, English Regency, and exotics from Imperial Russia also flocked to the new shop.

She may have been a contrarian, Madame Castaing, though perhaps she was merely one of those guileless persons who never pay attention to what they are supposed to like. Friends were told that her passion for nineteenth-century furnishings came from youthful reading of the novels of Balzac and Proust, with their detailed descriptions of rooms. What if other forward spirits exalted the eighteenth century or let themselves be seduced by the preciosities of art deco; Madame Castaing, who was far from poor, searched for treasure in the flea markets instead. (When her household things were put up for auction at Sotheby's in 2004, the most expensive offering was a pair of northern Italian serpent-headed chaise longues estimated at just under $20,000.) Castaing knew how to make captivating rooms with such stuff. She was also a discoverer of patterns and an idiosyncratic colorist (favoring especially robin's-egg blue, which found its way into her fabrics and onto her walls and lampshades). And once having turned up an object or a pattern she liked, she was quick to reproduce it and charge handsomely.

She was also notorious for her predilection for artificial flowers, which as she matter-of-factly explained, die less quickly than real ones. She herself became a thing of artifice eventually, and no one can say that her years were artificially shortened. Her installations at Rue Jacob, dating from the late 1940s, were allowed to gather dust (another oddity was her insistence on keeping dining tables set in perpetuity) and would acquire local celebrity for their great refusal of the housekeeping imperative. When you went through them, they made you think of museum displays, woefully maintained. She was loath, moreover, to part with her best-loved objects and perfectly prepared to frustrate a willing client. Madame kept private upstairs rooms on the premises that were hardly different from her showrooms; one domain bled into another. Our images are of her private bath and a conservatory. In the latter, dilapidated rattan contrasts strangely with the vigor of vines that have been left to themselves to grow as they would, for eons.

DUBLINERS

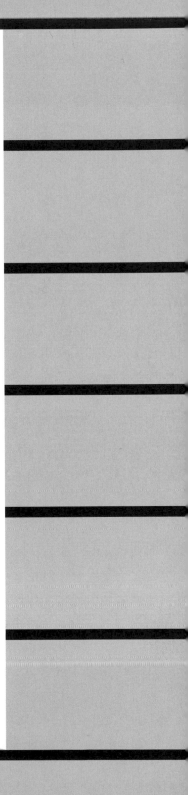

"A very strange young man." That's what Derry Moore has to say about Michael Casey, whom he photographed looking stern and spruce in the dress of a nineteenth-century British officer. The uniform came from Casey's personal collection. (Moore finds the colors in the portrait to be good.)

The image of Casey and those of his Dublin house date from 1991, the year the Celtic Tiger began to roar in earnest. You would never hear any echoes of the exotic Irish beast in these rooms, though. Something quite different was under way, a kind of excavation, as layers of paint, more here, fewer there, were peeled away. By means of this seemingly simple and straightforward process, the inscrutable past was being laid bare. Inscrutable, since precious little was to be read from the emerging motley patterns. You might look and you might wonder, that is all. Certainly Casey's handsomely planned house had been built during the eighteenth century, one imagines for an English family living in Dublin—at any rate, built for some family unlike the Caseys. Like Ireland itself, the house had fallen on hard times, been partitioned (like Ireland) to accommodate boarders, and its rooms painted over and over—always in another sober shade. How many such shades there were, how many to choose from!

One imagines this house reverberating, in 1991, with sounds made by Michael Casey's growing family, for the strange young man had purchased it to shelter a wife and children (two small ones at the time). Whatever scanty furnishings had been provided would scarcely have been enough to baffle their presence. (The very stair railings were gone, rendering passage up- or downstairs a tiny clattering adventure.) Certainly the atmosphere had grown theatrical, as if we should expect a bit of melodramatic business to commence in the dimness. Yet Casey, posing as an officer, was not about to embark on a soliloquy. No, he stands there, rapt for your attention, awaiting your admiration of his silent bearing. Was there even electricity? It is easy to think that glare would have been unwelcome to Michael Casey "Surely they had no radio or television," says Moore, and he may know as well as anyone.

There have been Bandinellis at Villa di Geggiano, near Siena, since 1527; things like the Reformation and the New World were breaking stories when they set up shop. The old family place has been remodeled only once, and for that you must go back to the waning eighteenth century. A chronic shortage of funds, more than anything, deserves credit for the survival of its wallpapers and frescoes for over two hundred years. However, the era of Antonioni and Fellini saw an actual restoration of Villa di Geggiano, for which an actual Bandinelli—and Marxist to boot—shall be remembered.

He must have been pleasingly complex, this Marxist scion. Count Ranuccio Bianchi Bandinelli (1900–1975) would become internationally known as a scholar of ancient Greece and Rome. He first felt the antiquarian passion in his backyard, in the presence of Etruscan ruins close by the ancestral home. No amount of politics would ever get in the way of his digging; somehow they went hand in hand. The soi-disant radical was only too happy to reclaim dispersed family furnishings for Villa di Geggiano, and today it is a virtual house museum commemorating his family's aristocratic ways in the years before the French Revolution. One might as well concede that the Bandinelli house supplies a fine object lesson for those who have never tasted the high life.

Our eccentric sampling of the interiors of Villa di Geggiano includes a rustic hall leading in from the garden entrance and the "conversation" room beyond, and from upstairs, two bedrooms and the central hall. Over the walls of the entrance hall (so immediately dark and cool after you step in from the heat and glare of outdoors) are frescoed pastel landscapes and peasants who could belong to Don Giovanni. These are the work of an itinerant Tyrolean painter, Ignazio Moder, and were applied in the year 1790. In the early days, guests were received in the weirdly elongated conversation room, really the "gossip" room, adjoining the hall. Here form would follow function, with women manning the banquette and men strolling or strutting before them, showing off calves snugly encased in silk. Nearing the gossip room, one still encounters a painted lady, on the door panel. She is Angelica, the pagan heroine of several Renaissance epics and the cause of more trouble for crusading Christian knights than any ordinary Saracen. The canopied beds upstairs illustrate a spindly, delightfully wayward Italian rococo. One of them, directly over the gossip room, offered regular shelter to the great liberal dramatist Vittorio Alfieri, who locals like to say was lazy to a fault; supposedly, he had to be chained to his desk by some rococo Bandinelli to write anything at all. The other bed reminds me of a yawning hippo, camouflaged by exactly matching wall patterns. Wallpaper in the upstairs hall (which the Bandinellis call their Blue Room) was hand-painted in France, circa 1780. Spared a grimmer fate, it buckles charmingly.

Another Spanish house to attract our photographer lies in Segovia, the Castilian stronghold best known today for its Roman aqueduct. This marvel has endured so very long without the help of mortar; mere congruence conspires with gravity to keep hewn stone blocks in place almost one hundred feet over Plaza del Azoguejo. During the Middle Ages, the citizens took their aqueduct for a holy miracle, and who shall say they were wrong? Most of the rest of Segovia is old, too. For the better part of five centuries, no urgency in the matter of business or trade has given cause to build or to demolish anything. Here even the city walls still stand. But it is scarcely surprising that historic structures are abandoned and left to decay, mortar or no.

You may gather from a glance that the house of the Marquesa de Lozoya, which looks toward the aqueduct, began life as a fortified tower. And that unlike other ancient buildings nearby, it is being well kept up. The Marquesa says that her family has lived in Segovia since the thirteenth century; such seems to be the age of her battlements. The house is a hybrid, for sure, whose quietly eventful architectural record appears in divers lesser exterior features borrowed from one style or another, in one age or the next. When you enter her front door, however, a new ambiance announces itself. If the frozen countenance of Segovia expresses the sternness of Spain in its time of greatness, the ingratiating austerities of the Marquesa's public rooms belong to the age of Stendhal. Her Yellow Salon might have been the backdrop for portraits by some hapless Ingres bottled up beneath the Pyrenees.

The rooms are Romantic in their way—playful reprises of ruder times. The Marquesa's double-story entrance hall in particular strikes the visitor as pretend-severe, its faux masonry mindful of the fortress theme and yet far removed. Gothic arches, with columns impossibly slender, figure in the pristine wallpaper of her dining room from circa 1815. And there is a certain contest underway, I find, between the ceilings, decorated with the shallowest Adamesque plasterwork, and plain naked floors below. The gold brocade lambrequin and portières for the doors leading out of the Yellow Salon—where the Marquesa could not play as a child—comprise an isolated gesture. Evidently, the slightest extravagance suffices for surroundings as alert as these are to the vibrations of fantasy. (Those versed in the ways of the world will insist that Sleeping Beauty Castle at Disneyland springs directly from Segovia's fairytale of an Alcázar).

TEN PLUS ONE FOR MONGIARDINO

Just imagine your house as ten plus one floors of a drawn-out right triangle, stacked. Well, not exactly a triangle, but something close enough. Each of your floors graduates in width from twelve feet or so at its spacious end down to around two at the pinched end opposite. Externally, from a certain charmed point of view, your house simply disappears like the edge of a razor. Meanwhile, within, on each of your ten plus one floors, the same dreadful pair of long walls (fifty and more feet they are) converge relentlessly, seeking their corner rendezvous. Luckily, the prospect is forestalled by flights of stairs wedged towards the narrow end of every floor, from the bottom to the uttermost top of your structure. Think of the monotony of the arrangement, ten plus one times over. Think of the climb.

Such a house (such a nightmare) confronted the great Milanese decorator Renzo Mongiardino late in his career. It had been built by an enterprising architect upon the odd scrap of land at his disposal on the edge of an already crowded block in Turin—that most surprising of Italian cities—some one hundred years before, to take in laboring families, one per floor. So many levels for living and laboring, all indistinguishable. Persons acquainted with Turin will have seen another, even stranger tower raised by the same man, Alessandro Antonelli, in the form of an immense heavy synagogue, part peristyle temple, which seems to hang from the sky by a fantastically tapering spire several hundred feet high. But we are concerned with his former tenement. This lesser wonder, after long and presumably honorable service, was acquired at last by a local motorcyclist playboy who naturally asked the great decorator to make of it an unexampled bachelor heaven.

Which he did, undoing the uniformity of the tenement, enabling the rich spectrum of activities envisioned by his client to unfold. The bizarre dreamlike proportions of its rooms lent themselves ever so readily to the staging of requisite fantasies. Two floors beneath the street, Mongiardino installed a Roman bath, windowless and spooky like a crypt. In the acute angle of the highest floor—destined to be the private quarters of the playboy—he lodged a gold-mosaic tub beneath walls stenciled in Ravenna blue. In the playboy's bedroom, the fireplace was valanced in antique damask trimmed with gold braid (borrowed from one of Mongiardino's own set decorations for a Zeffirelli film) and the damasked walls sheathed with white fabric, a sort of second skin. The dining room was meant to evoke "memories of tearooms, old cafés, small restaurants (mahogany, mirrors, colored glass), and, of course, the Caffè Florian" (Mongiardino, *Roomscapes*, 1993). Here the master of the house and his proud man posed for us (one no less in uniform than the other). As for the Milanese conjuror, he was weeks from death when he posed in that wonderful crypt-bath with marble flutings that let the steam condense and channel down to a concealed gutter. Incidentally, I do not see him trudging up and down the unending flights of stairs, but you know he certainly must have.

233

THINGS AND MORE (THINGS)

It is high-minded in here, so pluperfectly New England WASP. The backs of the chairs are upright, the decoration always chaste and dignified. The application of gilt is judicious. Bright striped silk upholstery winks at the visitor's second-and-a-half pluperfect martini; worthies in marble beam down from highboys or look on, soberly alas, from windowsills. The old China export trade appears to be alive and well. Whale oil would come in handy for a blackout. Books abound.

Little you see entered this world after Moby Dick, and still nearly everything shines and gleams. Somebody keeps busy, waxing and polishing and dusting, high and low. The beginnings of a tattered rug you may spy, but such signs of wear are exceptional. The proprietor, one suspects, cannot suffer from faded fortunes, or—to formulate the matter more completely—feels neither compelled nor especially eager to make a virtue of the threadbare and austere as do so many others of his class.

Upon second thought, there is a bit too much of everything in the Gomes home to qualify it as absolutely, pluperfectly New England WASP. A few too many silver chalices and bowls have been tucked away (or not); far too many prints queue up along the dining-room wall. (Yet everything manages to find its place.) And even where the rooms remain sparse, they may be just too plain pretty to serve as an advertisement for New England rectitude of the old school. Not even the architectural model of a church with steeple under glass, which has pride of place in the Gomes living room, is able to allay the suspicion.

The Reverend Gomes, Plummer Professor of Christian Morals and Pusey Minister in the Memorial Church, Harvard University, has written of his "unruly passion for things." As a child accompanying his mother, who from time to time supplemented the family income by cleaning the houses of established Yankee families, he became acquainted with the shabby gentility that often prevailed in them. The look of such a house, "whose essentially good bones wore well the ravages of time and neglect" was not to be achieved (he soon instinctively understood) "by the most zealous of decorators or collectors." It had come only as the "accumulation of generations of mixed taste and abilities, the whole of which was greater than the sum of its parts." Wisely, Reverend Gomes lives in the present, more or less ruling his passion, and in a house which is not, after all, pluperfectly New England WASP. (One might pronounce the Gomes residence "pluperflously" ditto.)

250

In keeping with standard practice, I confess to having inhabited these rooms forever (that's me, Carl Skoggard, on the bed with Otis). Living with a decorator-demiurge (let's call him "J") hasn't been easy, but you needn't worry about anyone bending your ear about it. No, what we have to deal with is the standard situation of before and after, courtesy of Derry Moore. The after images date from 2005, a truly addled moment in J's perpetual redecorating of our Madison Avenue apartment. The two remaining photographs must go back at least a dozen years. One shows the master bedroom in J's vast, absurdly vast, Baltimore apartment of yore (which I have characterized elsewhere as being nothing less than a tomb). The other is our Madison Avenue living room in its virgin dress, when J's residency in New York was still touch and go.

Nobody denies that as a decorator, J can venture boldly. Even so, to hear him tell it, in here he has been merely "cutting and pasting." And in a way he's right, for we are renters—the lowest of Gotham low. Apart from building in bookshelves and drawers, no structural alterations have been made to our home. J would have delighted in an elegant ensemble of rooms of course; no soul on earth treasures architectural integrity more. Yet he just goes on building up layer after layer in our dear old shoebox, or as he says, "cutting and pasting." Take the living-room ceiling. His new scheme accommodates an older one, hiding it in plain sight. That's how J manages everything: The smoke detector has been equipped with a fringe, and even my grand piano (banished) once wore a fetching tutu. Every bit of electrical wiring remains exposed, with variously hued strands looping and twisting as fancy prompts. After a leak damaged the crackle pattern traced on the living-room ceiling, J renewed the bad spots in a contrasting color, as if to commemorate the event. He says he got his idea from the Japanese, who mend their best ceramics with seams of gold. (Hiding in plain sight: I suppose that's how I got into the picture in the first place.)

Some people, apparently, find our New York rooms entertaining. Certainly they have been photographed enough. Indeed, every decorating twitch in this place has been documented in some credulous publication. Neither of us, however, knows of anything much that is really going on. As I see it, J is merely lathering up a "patina"— that favorite word of his—while trying to get comfortable in rooms that finally *are* comfortable. (In the old days he would joke that he was into "austere and inviting," and he was.) Whatever is genuinely new in the newest version of our apartment comes of J's sudden (and, seems to me, rather peculiar) desire to bring his objects into direct contact. To put it another way, he is no longer arranging flowers but mixing chemicals. He has begun assembling things that probably think of themselves as sculptures. Several of the strange creatures are lurking in the living room, but you have to look closely. (I particularly admire the way J has mounted his Ming scholar's rock inside a Bavarian rococo glass case so that it could topple over and smash a lineup of irreplaceable Christopher Dresser vases at any moment).

A WORD OF THANKS

My first thanks are to the owners, past and present, of the houses shown in this book and to those who created them.

I would also like to express special thanks to Princess Esra Jah, whose hospitality and kindness enabled me to see and photograph Hyderabad, in particular Falaknuma Palace, a magical place that retained the atmosphere of another age and where, mysteriously, fresh sheets continued to be laid on beds in which no one seemed to have slept since 1911. Likewise, I owe much to Señora de Urquijo, who opened the doors of the Marqués de Casa Torres's great house in Madrid; living alone except for various aging servants and surrounded by Goyas, El Grecos, Zurbaráns, and even a very fine Velázquez, the Marqués embodied upper-class Spanish life as it must have been in the early years of the twentieth century.

The following individuals deserve the lion's share of credit for the creation of *Rooms*: Joseph Holtzman, who had the original idea for the book, selected most of its material from my archive a decade ago, and with his unerring eye dictated its layout and appearance; Charles Miers, publisher of Rizzoli USA, who commissioned *Rooms* and provided both stimulus and reassurance; Rizzoli's gracious and dedicated managing editor, Ellen Nidy; and Carl Skoggard, who has produced texts of Proustian elegance and subtlety. (My only worry is that readers might be put off by his far too generous introduction, which made me feel as if I were reading the most charitable obituary of myself.)

My thanks are also due to Tom Beckham for his sensitive typography and all-around graphics wizardry and to Paul B. Franklin, who coordinated every aspect of the project with formidable efficiency.

There is one other person I must thank, someone who over the years has had a great influence on my work. Paige Rense, as editor of *Architectural Digest*, commissioned so many of the photographs in this book. Her perception and vision in appreciating the importance of places such as Falaknuma at a time when their significance eluded others provided me with encouragement that I cannot begin to repay.

—Derry Moore